D0053306

be happy.

A little book to help you
live a happy life.

be happy.

A little book to help you
live a happy life.

by Monica Sheehan

RUNNING PRESS
PHILADELPHIA · LONDON

For Andrew Kroon

We love you always

Library of Congress Control Number: 2006930239

ISBN 13: 978-0-7624-2962-2

Conceived, written, and illustrated by Monica Sheehan
Produced exclusively for Running Press Book Publishers by:
Herter Studio
432 Elizabeth Street
San Francisco, CA

This book may be ordered by mail from the publisher.
Please include $2.50 for postage and handling.
But try your bookstore first!

Running Press Book Publishers
2300 Chestnut Street
Philadelphia, Pennsylvania 19103-4371

Visit us on the web!
www.runningpress.com

many thanks to:

Jon Anderson
Andrew Clarke
Caroline Herter
Debbie Berne
Suzy McCabe
Tina Klem
Mike Hubert
Margaret Sheehan
Kara, Jack, and Meredith
Sarah Kroon Chiles
My brother Andrew
and his bright boys, Eamon & Emmett
Al Ellenberg
Eddie McCrossin
Kevin Byrne and his garden
My Sisters:
Mary Jane, Ann, Nora, and Sarah

Show up.

Follow your heart.

Stay inspired.

Stop being
a victim.

Do things you're
good at.

Love your work.

Get a new
perspective.

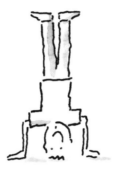

Have a sense
of wonder.

Don't isolate.

Find people
you love.

Set goals.

Finish what
you started.

TAP
TAP

Help others.

Do a one day
news fast.

Dance.

Pamper yourself.

Face your fears.

Go to a museum.

Any decision is better
than no decision.

Exercise.

Limit television.

Listen to music.

Get in touch
with nature.

Lighten up.

Have a moral compass.

Get a good
night's sleep.

Read books.

Buy yourself flowers.

Reach out.

Set up a
realistic schedule.

Don't compare yourself
with others.

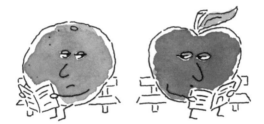

Live in the moment.

PAST   FUTURE

Don't beat
yourself up.

Accept that life
has its
ups and downs.

Every night reflect
on the 'good' things
about your day.

Be open to
new ideas.

Believe in yourself.

Be kind.

Let people know
how special they are.

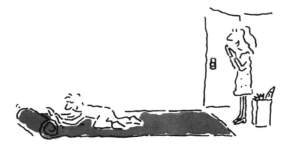

Be honest
with yourself.

Don't focus on
negative thoughts.

Focus on creating
what you desire.

Make time just
to have fun.

Say thank you to the people
who teach you, support you,
encourage you,

and get you
a cup of coffee.

Don't forget...
money doesn't
buy happiness.

Give away what you
don't need,
to someone who does.

Value who you are
right now.

Be part of
a community.

Find a
common ground.

Keep the romance
in your life.

Make a
gratitude list.

Love your Mother Earth.

Do your best.

Don't lose hope.

(You never know what
tomorrow will bring.)

TODAY

TOMORROW

Keep learning.

Want what
you have.

Believe in something bigger than yourself.

Stay close to
friends and family.

Be true to yourself.